BITS AND PIECES

ACKNOWLEDGEMENTS

I would like to thank my Lord and Savior Jesus Christ for giving me the strength, knowledge, and wisdom I need in order to travel this road and journey. I've learned to walk through my fears. I also would like to thank with my whole heart my daughters Samika, Brianna and Kabrina for believing in me and their love and support. Thank you to all of my friends and family and your kind words and feedback. To all my social media followers, thank you for all your likes, loves and comments.

SON
(Dedication)

My Son,
I carry you in between each of my heartbeats
I carry you in my spirit
You left,
but you never left me.
I love you forever.

INTRODUCTION

I didn't set out to write a book, I set out to survive. For most of my life, I carried pieces of myself in silence. The fat kid trying to disappear, the daughter of an alcoholic, the woman bruised by those that said they love her, the girl who was taught to endure rather than speak. But somewhere in the middle of all the chaos I started writing things down. Little bits. Little pieces, parts of memories, emotions and truths that I was afraid to say out loud. Bits and Pieces is the sound of a woman learning to hear herself for the first time. It's my way of making sense of the life I've lived and maybe, in reading it, you'll find pieces of your own story too. I don't write as an expert, I write as a witness to pain, to growth, to the moments that nearly broke me. This is for the broken girls. The voiceless ones. The Survivors. The ones still piecing themselves together.

Welcome to my truth....

"I always felt like the black sheep because I lacked something, and then I discovered I was the black sheep because I carried something... I was made this way for a reason."

I write, I cry
I write, I cry
For all my words I do not lie
And for every hello,
and every goodbye
I write I cry, I write I cry

UNTITLED

Years of anger built up inside
From some things I had to hide
Because of other people's pride
And from this mental ride
I wanted to commit suicide
And to my own self I lied
And over and over continuously denied
Myself of a truly happy life

"Abuse, confusion, whispered lies.
The echo of whispered cries"

SECRETS

The first memory that pops into my mind is when I was somewhere between 5 and 6 years old, a man that I choose not to disclose tried to force my head down on his penis. I still remember what it smelled like. All the while my Mom and Dad were downstairs watching tv. He never quite got my mouth on it but it swept across my face. I took off running and when I got downstairs I jumped into a chair. I was so scared and my Mom and Dad never noticed the fear. I thought I would get a whooping if I said something. Wow how fucked up is that?

I am no Psychiatrist or therapist, but I would say this incident is the start of what the rest of my life would be like. It was the start of secrets, the first secret in my life, a secret that I kept from my parents for over 20 years. A secret that I would one day wish I kept from my dad forever.

"I was taught that love was something to survive. That trust was earned through pain. That being used was simply being wanted. Every touch felt borrowed. And every word was dressed as comfort."

ARGUMENTS

My childhood was shaped by the shadow of my parent's relationship. My Mom was codependent of my Dad and connected to him in ways that made her powerless. My Dad, an alcoholic, carried his anger like a weapon waving it in his drunken rages that seemed endless. His words cut deep, his voice always raised, his presence always heavy. I remember mommy and daddy arguing all the time, especially when Daddy was drinking. I would sit at the top of the stairs peaking through the banisters and could hear every word. The loudness and name calling; bitch, motherfucker, asshole, dummy, stupid, fuck you, you ain't shit and believe me there is so much more. Sometimes the arguments became physical and as a child it was hard to process.

The smell of alcohol so stale
Every Friday night without fail
The darkness,
the sadness,
The silence,
the fear,
The rage, the anger, the arguing
The fights all night
Going deeper within to hide
To see or not to hear
All the while feeling every emotion
Continuously over and over
Month after month,
year after year,
I still cry those tears

RAGING

Being called stupid or dumb was the norm. Every week it was the same shit, and every day was the same, week in and week out. It started on Thursdays which was daddy's paydays and was also the days he came home with the little brown bag and you knew hell was coming with it. After a while of drinking he would start saying things like, "Ain't none of y'all shit", "you just like your momma", "get your ass out of my house", and that's just a little bit of the rage. He would finish the whole fifth and then pass out on the couch.

Only God knows how he would make it to work the next morning and you knew that evening around 4:00 he was going to walk through the back door with that brown bag in his hands and hell coming with him. Here we go again.

"I am shaped by the shadows of your drunkenness, your loud voice of words, cutting me deep, rendering me powerless. I struggle with love and hate"

EQUATE

Sometimes I walk through life
Not knowing when I am being done wrong
Because disrespect is the norm
And in the midst of the storm
I equate love with pain
On my pillow my teardrop stains
Because your energy still remains
and I have everything to lose
and nothing to gain
But I refuse for it all to be in vain
And still the meaning is the same
I equate love with pain

"I am the afterthought,
The one who wasn't good enough the first time,
The used, the abused, then left confused
I paid my dues."

REASONS

I was not allowed to have feelings,
or to make my feeling known
How to love or to be loved properly,
I was never shown
To love or to be loved never lasts long
This is why I walk this earth alone

My Dad used to always say that I was not allowed to have my own thoughts or feelings nor did my opinion matter. This always made me feel worthless, like I was nothing or nobody. I was pretty much invisible because no one could see me, or what I was going through. Writing made me feel free. Free to be me.

From the thought in my mind
To the truth and the lies
From the emotions I feel
To the things of or against my will I am giving my word a voice
It's the sleepless nights in bed
And the noises in my head
It's the countless tears I've cried
From being forced to put my feelings aside This is why I made the choice
And decided to give my words a voice

My father was the most influential person in my life and growing up under that roof left a mark on me. I believe that my choices in men are all based upon my relationship with my dad. Every man I've encountered since has worn a piece of his traits. His anger, his charm, and his brokenness. They resurface in the faces and actions of those I let into my life. It's as if I'm searching for something familiar, something that feels like him, even if it's painful. My father's shadow has lingered, shaping the way I love, trust, and understand the world.

24

FAMILIAR SOUL

My heart was tainted a long time ago
Somewhere in my childhood
I forget how many years old
Hidden and kept secret
my story was never told
Every man I've met is a familiar soul

"Validate me,
Approve me,
See me,
Love me
NOT"

FRAGMENTS OF ME

I write my life in fragments,
Bits and pieces of who I've been,
Woven with shadows of who I might have been.
My mother a quiet connection to chaos,
My father, a storm that never calmed.
His words, like sharp pieces of glass,
That cut through the silence,
Through her and through me
The men who followed
Wore his face in different ways,
Their hands, their voices,
Echoes a ghost I never asked to know,
I was taught love was something to survive
That trust was earned through pain,
That being used was simply being wanted
Every touch felt borrowed,
Every word was a blade dressed as comfort.
And I still rise in the pieces.
Each one holds a truth,
a scar,
a scream,
a whispered plea.
I put them together with ink,
With the soul of my poems
Because even broken stories deserve to be told
I am not whole
But I am here

AIN'T THAT A BITCH

I have spent over 30 years navigating through relationships. Yet intimate they were all unsuccessful. There were no engagements, no wedding rings, no promise rings, and no future in any of them. A lot of my work is built on those loves, losses and experiences.

One of the things that I have come to realize is that with the men that I have let come into my life, I hold on way longer than I should, especially when I know deep down inside that it's over. I believe it comes from growing up the way that I did and the things I witnessed over time in my mom and dad's marriage. I realize I was always trying to prove myself because I never felt good enough.

Imagine not only experiencing verbal abuse at home but also at school from my teacher, I should add my math teacher around the 7th grade. She was very mean to me. I will never forget her. She was worse than my dad every day I went to class she called me stupid and dumb if I asked a question or didn't understand something, I would sit in the back of the class hiding from her, but she would always find me and make me go the blackboard to solve a problem and she knew I didn't know how to do it. She called on me anyway and would embarrass me and call me names in front of everyone. I decided to tell my mom this particular day and she asked my dad to go to the school. I was glad because I thought he was really going to tell her off but instead he agreed with her and told her she should keep calling me names because I deserved it and needed it because I shouldn't be so stupid and so she did. Once again "Pain".

My mom was the good wife who carried the weight that he could not. Though he was the man of the house she led everything. Every single day she did everything for him. She kept the house spotless, cooked his meals, washed and ironed his clothes and still worked as a sheet metal worker for forty years. She hardly rested and never complained. But I felt her exhaustion. I saw the way the weight pressed down on her. She gave so much and received so little in return. His words cut her down, sometimes his presence drained her and I suffered right along with her. Every insult, every dismissal, every cruel remark, I felt because some were aimed at me too. She took care of him till his last breath, just as she always did. She was unwavering, even after a lifetime of sacrifice and mistreatment. I watched it all, I carried it all, And I still feel it.

"I am Her, I am she, I am I, I am Me"

ME

Memories of the day we met
And so many promises that you set
And all those things I did expect
But never did I suspect
nor did I think you would ever neglect
"ME"
So few truths and so many lies
All while looking into my eyes
You were scheming my demise
Dressed up in your smiling disguise
You were planning your goodbyes
to "ME"
Never did I want to see
What was really in front of me
All your malice and deceit
I feel so much defeat
But in this game you played for keeps
And now you will always own a part of "ME"
Now each and everyday
I get on my knees and pray
Looking forward to a brighter day
But never again to my dismay
Shall I ever have such a big price to pay
For just being "ME"

NO NAME

Have you ever woke up a no name
With nothing to lose and nothing to gain
There was no glory, there was no fame
Only your guilt and only your shame
And it turns out it was all a game
And you were just a no name

"They said I was different, but what they really meant was I was less like them, less important, less to love, or less to hold space for, but I wasn't meant to blend in I was meant to stand out."

LEFT BEHIND

Every thought,
Every choice,
Every moment and every emotion was a burden
There was no peace and there was no purpose
There was just me and my mind stuck in an abyss
Falling to my death from your poisonous kiss
In which I do not miss
And I can't deny
That I was stuck in the dark space wondering why
You left me

The definition of trauma is a deeply distressing or disturbing experience.
Well, I carry my traumas deep in my soul.
I wear them like I wear my clothes.
I put them on and take them off daily.
It's my everyday norm.

"It's OK to be Beautifully out of place."

MENTAL PRISON

I've lived a life so dark and deep,
And in this life I shall reap
And there is so much I have not done
Because I am stuck in a mental prison
How do I escape this lock and key
Because this is life or death for me
No laughter I hear, no sun I see
And now I'm back at the beginning
No one to protect me
So I just checked out,
I am stuck in this place of turmoil and self doubt
No place to hide or nowhere to run,
I am stuck in this mental prison

"I dance with the dark, it knows my name
Whispers my wounds
and dresses my shame
And I wear it all like art
Now the whole world can see
my broken parts"

MY FIRST TIME

I kept telling myself I don't feel, I don't feel
But I know it's real
It's long, it's hard, it hurts
It's my first time
Which defined my all time
To like hurts
To love hurts
To fuck hurts
I've been being penetrated my whole life
I am scared, I am confused
I've been used, abused,
Treated harshly, Made fun of,
Laughed at, cheated on, lied to, lied on,
I've been wronged
Nothing but pain and shame
This is not a game
It's my life
My whole life

"I will be me and do me for myself and no one else. Because I am more than meets the eye and undeniable in my true self."

I LOVE LOVE

I love love, and love loves me
A bond that I carry very deeply
It wraps me in it's warm embrace
A gentle touch,
a quiet place
I see love in the light
In whispered dreams that fills my night
It's in my heart, it's in my soul
A force that makes my broken pieces whole
Love loves me on my best days
And through the dark it finds it way
It lifts me high and sets me free
I love love and love loves me

"My resilience doesn't define me. My humanness does."

CONNECTION

Two people attracted to each other,
has some Similarities
And some are because they share quite a few Familiarities
Like alcohol, drugs, trauma, and abuse.
Could that be the thing that connects the two?
Are those the things that connect me and you?

"I am the fire and the cold. Forced to watch your lies unfold. No lies I have ever told. This shit done got old."

BROKEN

I live in poetry,
in my bits and pieces,
in my broken pieces,
in my shattered pieces
Held together by strands of hope
And fear that lie in the creases
No longer connected or meshed together
Are those broken sharp pieces that are lost forever
I will never get those back

"It's as if I am drawn to his chaos. Trying to fix
something that's not even mine."

MARRIED

I was caught in your rapture so deep
And all the while knowing
you were not mines to keep
Wrapped up in your marital non bliss
Fooled by your words and your pretentiousness
You fooled me once and you fooled me twice
I knew what I was in for
And I still rolled the dice
Playing this game of russian roulette
I learned that in the end
You get, what you get

"Time is moments promised that you don't keep.
Messing with my time is messing with my peace."

TIME

Let's talk about time
Time is everything
Time is the end all to the be all
Time is your winter,
your spring,
your summer
and your fall
Time is the moments promised that you don't keep
Time is the sleepless nights you promised to make love to
me
but don't
You know you can't make that up, that moment was
missed,
it's gone
And once again I'm stuck here all alone hanging in time
It's lonely sitting in time
Because that's when you suddenly realize
That everyday you wasted and all that's been lost
People say time doesn't cost but it does
That's what time spent,
spend time,
time lost,
time costs means
So while spending time
you were just baiting me
And all the while I was losing my mind,
losing me
And just like that our situation ran out of time.

EXONERATED

Tired of looking at life thru past tense eyes
All the pain,
all the lies
All the people I despise
The severed ties
and the "me oh my's"
The guilt,
the shame,
the heavy cry's
And the hurtful goodbyes
From the living to those that died
"I forgive you"

" I realize now that no matter how much my heart yearns or how much my soul burns, I am really not your concern."

NO CONCERN

Lines crossed, Boundaries broken
Heart shattered, words unspoken
My heart yearns my soul burns
I guess I am not your concern

"I am the fat girl who lived, loved, and wrote it all down."

THE FAT KID

I grew up the fat kid, the easy target, the punch line The one that everybody would point at, laugh at and whisper about as if I couldn't hear. But I did. You hear everything when you are a fat kid. You memorize all of it, you carry it home like it's your homework.

At home there was no escape. Not from the world and not from my dad. He never ever called me fat, but his words hurt me deeper than that with things like, "DUMB", "STUPID" or questions like "Who told you to think?" or "Didn't I tell you, you ain't talking about nothing?"

It was as if my thoughts were nothing but trash that you could just throw away. I was a big girl with a shrinking soul, apologizing for my thoughts before I even had them, and he would look through me as if I wasn't there. I became just the afterthought. I was a body that took up space in the room with a voice that was too small to even matter.

But I mattered. Even when they said I didn't, even

when I believed every word they all said about me. There was something inside of me that was whispering to me under all of the shame which is why I am speaking for the fat kid today. No one gets to tell me I am too much, but not enough at the same time. I write for her, the fat kid, I write for me because I carried it all and I still stand.

It's funny how people only see your bounce back but not the bruises and how they praise the climb without understanding the toll it took on you from the fall. I've been celebrated for surviving while they never paid attention to the fact that I was breaking inside. Falling apart piece by piece. They would say things like "Girl you are so strong" like that is the only thing worth seeing about me.

I am more than the things that I have survived, and I realize that there is a power in being whole, broken, healing, and hurting all at the same time.

I am not here to be a lesson, a symbol, or even a story of strength. I am here because I breathe, I feel, I fall short, and I try again, and all of that is enough. My resilience got me through it all, but my humanness is what makes me worth knowing.

SISTERS

I have sisters. But sometimes it feels like I only have the word sisters, not the bond, not the closeness, not a real connection. We were raised in the same house but we were not raised the same way. We have different versions of what the same household was like. People assume that siblings are cut from the same cloth, and that if you share the same blood, a roof, and parents, you must've had the same childhood. But that's a lie, a very dangerous one. Because it erases all the cracks in the floorboards and all the memories, and all the experiences we each shared differently and all the ways love or lack thereof landed on each of us. Me and my sisters shared the same dad but got different versions of him. Funny thing is, it took me years to learn that when we shared our thoughts about the past, though different, we were all telling the truth even when our truths did not align. We are sisters and we need to hold hands, not grudges. We need not judge one another but love each other and accept one another just the way we are. We weathered the storm.
All of us girls. Same blood. Different bruises.

"I wanna take a moment to share how deep this shit goes Pain so deep it's ripping through my soul. The love I have for you only God knows."

DEEP

I was told that I love too deep
And wounds like mine are hard to keep
But I hear their voices in my sleep
The ones I lost and the ones I keep
I guess I do love too deep

"I've learned that sometimes the Why is unimportant. In the end you realize after the pain and the suffering, that it really had nothing to do with you."

FOR MY FATHER

I love you Daddy and I know you loved me. I know now that you were a broken man and that your brokenness started in your childhood as well. I spent years trying to figure out why I was never good enough, smart enough, or just enough and now I realize you were carrying your own bruises and that you never got what you needed as well. Daddy this is not about blame, this is about release. I have always loved you even when it hurt, even when I just didn't understand. I know you did the best you could. I carry you dad not just in my pain but in my stubbornness and my fire and the strength you unintentionally gave me. I forgive you daddy and I free you and I free myself.

ABOUT THE AUTHOR

Janice Traylor is a writer, poet, and truth-teller whose work gives voice to the quiet, painful, and powerful moments that shape our lives. Born and raised in a working class household, Janice grew up navigating the complexity of family, survival, and silence. Her debut book, Bits and Pieces, is a deeply personal collection of poetry that explores childhood trauma, body image, love, identity, and healing.

Through her storytelling, Janice reclaims the narrative of a black woman who has endured emotional, and verbal abuse and lived to turn pain into purpose. She is the founder of BIT&PIECES, a brand that celebrates individuality and resilience through words, and everyday expression. Janice believes in the beauty of broken things and the power of putting them back together.

www.ingramcontent.com/pod-product-compliance
Lightning Source LLC
Chambersburg PA
CBHW061318120626
46546CB00007B/2643